D1223414

RACHEL ASHWELL

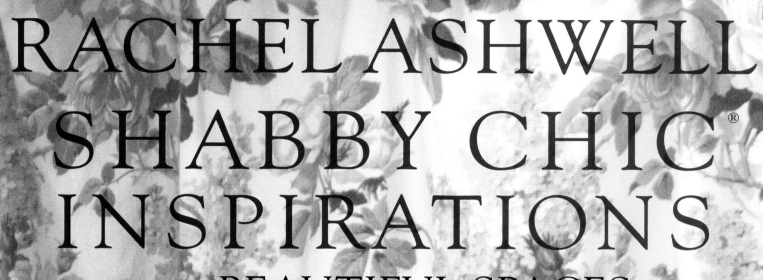

RACHEL ASHWELL
SHABBY CHIC®
INSPIRATIONS
AND BEAUTIFUL SPACES

CICO BOOKS

LONDON NEW YORK

BOCA RATON PUBLIC LIBRARY
BOCA RATON, FLORIDA

Published in 2011 by CICO Books
an imprint of Ryland Peters & Small

20–21 Jockey's Fields
London WC1R 4BW

519 Broadway, 5th floor
New York, NY10012

10 9 8 7 6 5 4 3 2 1

Text © Rachel Ashwell 2011
Design and photography © CICO Books 2011
(photographs on pages 52–59 © Patrick Cline/Lonny and
pages 168–179 © Trevor Tondro)

The author's rights have been asserted. All rights
reserved. No part of this publication may be reproduced,
stored in a retrieval system, or transmitted in any form or
by any means, electronic, mechanical, photocopying, or
otherwise, without the prior permission of the publisher.

A CIP catalog record for this book is available from the
Library of Congress and the British Library.

ISBN 978 1 907563 59 1

Printed in China

Specially commissioned photography: Gisela Torres

Text: Alexandra Parsons
Editor: Gillian Haslam
Design: Roger Hammond, bluegumdesigners
Additional photography: pages 1, 11 left and right,
180–181, 190 center: Amy Neunsinger; pages 52–59:
Patrick Cline/Lonny; pages 168–179: Trevor Tondro;
page 189: Dusty Lu

contents

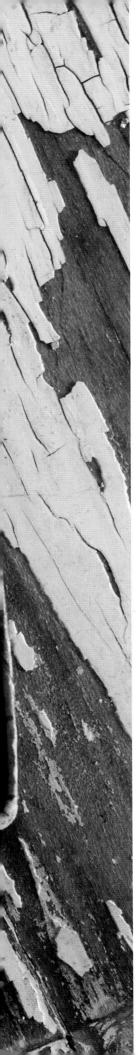

dedication

It was a lucky day for me when...

When Jaimee Seabury crossed my path and took care of everything in my working world so that I could focus on what I love to do, including this book.

When Cindy, David, Gillian, Sally, Roger, Alex, and all at CICO agreed to do another book with me, and Gisela said yes to shooting it.

When Sera, Brendan, Huw, Emma, Pearl, Hannah and James, Sophie, Sandy, and Sharon let me into their beautiful, inspiring domains.

When my children became adults and sources of inspiration for me.

When I pondered just how many friends and associates are in my life and support me so (including all at Rachel Ashwell Shabby Chic Couture).

And the luckiest of all was when I realized that having art in our soul gives us all a forever safe place in minds.

And for that I am so thankful.

introduction

In my world, inspiration is the core ingredient needed for design, and inspirational design can be truly life changing. When I see a blank canvas or an empty room, I see an opportunity to create a story. Often my starting point is to reflect through my inspirational bible. I have always considered myself a romantic at heart, having built a business over 20 years with romance as the core visual aesthetic. Romantic movies, music, and poetry are my constant source of inspiration. Sometimes it is specific elements I see in a movie or hear in a song that I fold into the visuals of my storytelling, but usually it is more about a feeling I want to capture in my work.

My bed and breakfast, "The Prairie by Rachel Ashwell", is part aesthetic inspiration from *Marie Antoinette*, part authentic detail from *Coal Miner's Daughter*, and part passion from *Gone with the Wind*. The Prairie is my Tara. And my deep-rooted love of country music now has a home—pure poetry.

My brief stay in my Notting Hill apartment fed me the fantasy of Peter Pan and Wendy, with Mozart or Pavarotti as background music for a rainy winter's day. I find inspiration in movies like *Wuthering Heights*, *Bright Star*, and *Out of Africa*, music from country to opera, and places like Beatrix Potter's Hill Top house and John Keats' house. Absorbing these movies and getting lost in the songs help me create the tapestry of my work. If one is inspired by the works of others, it is not to

say that our visions are not original and from our own souls; but absorbing other artists' stories and expressions adds dimensions to our creativity on a much deeper level, bringing Technicolor and stereo sound to our work. I believe that by exploring how artists work with color, space, and juxtapositions, it can open us up to new ideas that can become our own, depending on how we interpret them. It is easy for us as artists to stay in our comfort zones, and sometimes it is hard for others to see us in new ways. The key is for our unique common thread to stay present.

In this book I was very open to exploring new ways to express my stories. Some darker rooms and palettes are present, but in my eyes they are still light rooms in spirit but perhaps richer in depth and with a beauty I would not have been open to

in the past. I am at a stage of my life where I am able to be more "present" due to my curiosity and willingness to fully experience all there is about where I am.

Each and every room in this book is like a visual poem to me. Some of the poetry is woven from the design of the homes, some from the artisans' creations, and some from the stated values of home and family. The homes within this book all have many layers of beauty and inspiration to absorb. I was inspired, moved, and intrigued by the homes I was invited into. I was able to explore not just the homes, but all the nooks and corners. I found little treasures of character that were extensions of the owners' creative expression. This was an important element for me to discover and reveal along with the more obvious beauty.

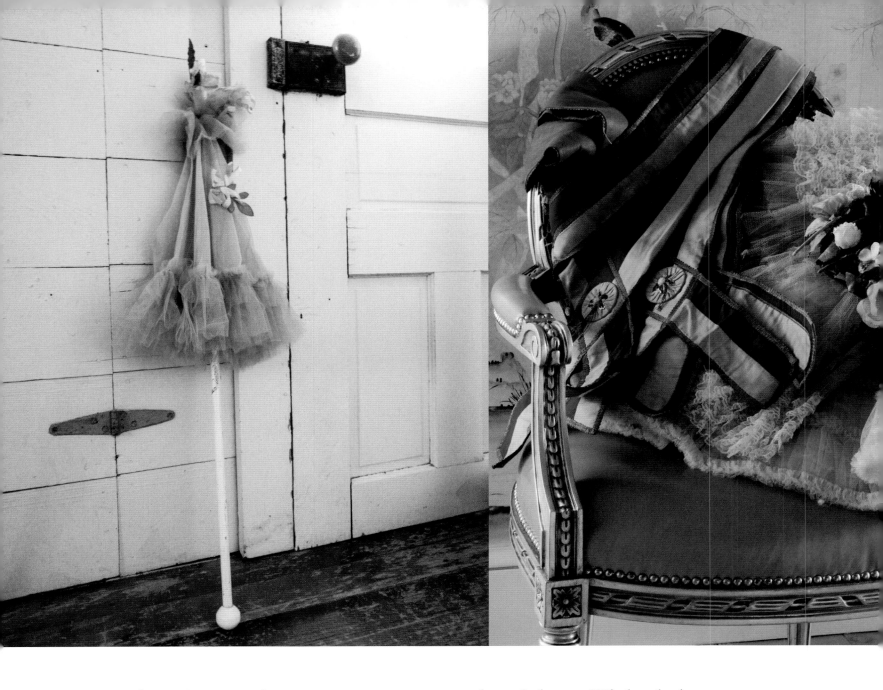

Interior design is a much more intimate journey than fashion. While clothing can influence an attitude, it is an external layer, with the purpose of showing ourselves to others. A home is our intimate space where things are not necessarily seen by others or perfect but it is where we create our art, we go inward, we build our nest and family values, refresh our souls and spirits.

Each one of the homes in this book is all soul and passion, created by people who have the common thread of creating art as their way of telling their stories authentically. Some stories are large and take up space, some are teeny but nonetheless meaningful, and require a discerning eye to create and discover. These twelve homes were rich, light, bright, and wonderful places to be. I relate

to the values and true sense of the words "handmade with love." Many Rachel Ashwell Shabby Chic Couture products go through many steps of the human touch—hand-dyed, handstitched, handpicked—before becoming complete. It adds true value and creates future heirlooms.

The beauty of art is that we all see different aspects that inspire us, so inspiration and design keep going and going; we inspire and we are inspired. I find when I let my thoughts and mindset live in a space of creativity, life is good and a safe place to be.

texas belle

Previous page: The front steps of Liliput Lodge, a screened-in porch, and me. Lush green landscapes and huge skies—my prairie dream. Warm winds dry laundry in minutes, making a poetic sight in the process. Little wooden structures are purposely scattered around the property.

Left: Wisteria grows gracefully and delicately, bringing a feminine element to cowboy country. Round Top, Texas, doesn't do florists' shops or bouquets. Garden and wild flowers in mason jars are the signature floral statement.

Opposite: I have always loved the "Grapes of Wrath" element of a screened-in porch—always a little dusty, but a quiet ambiance inspiring storytelling in rocking chairs.

the prairie

Round Top, Texas, is a tiny town about 75 miles from Austin and 85 from Houston. The moment I get in my pick-up truck at Austin airport and put on my country music—Willie Nelson's "On The Road Again" or John Denver's "Country Roads"—I feel "home." The small settlement has a population of 81 that swells to tens of thousands during "antique weeks" and other art festivities throughout the year. I have been coming to the flea markets here for many years—I always leave with an abundance of treasures—and staying at The Outpost at Cedar Creek was always part of this sacred experience. The rustic tranquillity and the yummy breakfasts were perfection. A few months ago, The Outpost was for sale and, on what might have seemed like a whim, I became the new owner, and my long-held dream of having a small, perfect hotel became real.

Opposite: A bedroom in Blue Bonnet Barn. The room is very rustic, and the combination of a ditsy floral print and a linen-upholstered headboard bring a balance of comfort. Delicate curtain panels threaded onto slim brass rods diffuse the Texas sunshine, which enters the room obliquely. I paid great attention to the curtains, buying up as many sets of vintage panels as I could for all the rooms.

Right: Laundry rooms and linen cupboards are always favorite, sacred spaces for me. Each building has its own labeled shelf with a pile of Rachel Ashwell Shabby Chic Couture bedding, all housed in Liliput Lodge. The beauty of my design is that it lends itself to mismatching.

cowboy country with frills

There is so much to love and appreciate about this little piece of heaven. The main Homestead house was built in the 1800s. Over time other properties have been transplanted here from nearby lands. The previous owner of The Outpost at Cedar Creek was Lenore Prudhomme; with Danny Reibling, she painstakingly found, moved, and restored every structure. Along with my purchase, I inherited a true labor of their love, and I plan to cherish every element. My goal was, and will continue to be, to add my luxurious and sumptuous aesthetic and make it feel authentic within this world. Upgrading plumbing and installing signature furnishings, beds, and bedding from Rachel Ashwell Shabby Chic Couture was my first priority.

my little house on the prairie

The legacy of Lenore's labor of love continues as I took up the reins of transforming The Outpost into The Prairie. The soul of Texas seemed to resonate with many and soon I found myself with a dedicated, passionate team. During the renovation period each person was careful to protect all the wonderful authentic elements and just layer in our values of beauty, comfort, and function. Every corner, every vista is poetry and a delight to the eye.

Left and opposite: Dappled sunlight filters through a pretty vintage remnant tacked to the window frame. Even with graffitied dark plank walls and brick floors, the claw-foot tub and an abundant shower curtain bring such romance to this little authentic en-suite bathroom in Blue Bonnet Barn.

Overleaf: A bedroom in Meadow Manor. Here I embraced a slightly formal feel and installed pink-and-white striped wallpaper by Farrow & Ball. Shimmering beige silk dupion curtains contributed to the grown-up and refined aesthetic. However, the original worn floorboards and distressed chandelier added a timeworn patina where cowboy boots can still feel at home. Even in a bed-and-breakfast, storage space is important, but it's often not built into these old houses, so I plopped a small cupboard on top of a dresser and made a kind of armoire.

Below: French embroidered lace panels paint lovely shadows.

Below right: Old jam jars, roses, and wisteria.

Previous page and opposite: I inherited the deep-colored damask wallpaper and, surprising myself, I decided to let it stay as the backdrop to the room. Layering overstuffed Rachel Ashwell Shabby Chic Couture sofas with formal velvet teal gilt chairs gives a mushy comfort to a slightly formal, albeit well-trodden, room. Taxidermy is part of Texas ranch culture, and while I am never likely to buy any, I did decide to embrace those that came with the property, and honored them into my world with floral hats and crowns. The lampshade frame, restored lace curtains, table chandelier, faded chintz shades, chipped mirrors and tables, and glamorous roses in a jam jar all paint the picture of the shabby and the chic.

Marie Antoinette comes to Texas

In the same way I have brought the shabby into chic for two decades, at The Prairie I am embracing the diversity of my aesthetics, while still keeping my common threads. The charmingly worn and wonky, the distressed and recycled share space comfortably with delicate gilt wood French empire chairs, feminine fabrics, crystal chandeliers with silk shades, and always a bit of bling. Serving high teas, special snacks, and feasts will give me the opportunity to let my collection of vintage china come into play. At The Prairie I am able to tell my creative stories: everything I have learnt and honed over the past two decades in design has come to fruition here. In a way this is my showcase, my legacy. My little houses on the prairie…

Left: Liliput Lodge can be rented by the room or as a whole, when house guests can use this gem of a kitchen. Authentic distressed cupboards, a butler's sink, and zinc worktops are a still-life painting. Initially I planned to replace the original light fixture with a crystal chandelier, but leaving well alone was another opportunity for me to balance the true original aesthetics with my typical signature. The little table with yummy legs is a flea-market find. I had been clutching onto the pale pink valance for the longest time and, voila, it fits perfectly across the window.

Far left: I prettified the two inherited chairs with some linen seat cushions. Now they are ready to welcome flea-market shoppers or guests wanting The Prairie experience in the Lone Star State.

Clockwise from left: Ready for big little Texas meals. The Prairie china collection. Repurposed wine bottles and jars are signature vases in cowboy country. Broken angel wings, a country song waiting to happen, signify still being able to soar though life, even when seemingly fragile.

Left: We can comfortably sleep 16 at The Prairie but with our luxurious feather-topped spare mattresses, we can put up quite a few extras. The Rangers Lounge is where we serve food. It is a beautiful mishmash of a corrugated tin ceiling and salvaged wood walls. Patina, texture, natural light, and lovely views from all windows make this a breathtaking place to be.

Opposite: The cloakroom was graced with my favorite-ever vintage wallpaper which I found online, and a sturdy wooden armchair was given a new reason for living—it will see a few more tomorrows.

Previous page: The "magic hour." In early spring, foliage lies dormant, soon to blossom and burst into splendor. The classic Texan twig furniture came with the property—I added some pink floral country cushions. Perfect bliss.

Opposite: Ornately embroidered linen panels, simply applied to the windows and doorway. A dusty blue painted trim adds romance and femininity to counterbalance the land of cowboys.

Right: My uniform pastel wraps are hitched to a post.

TIMEWORN ELEGANCE

Previous page: A falling-apart Fortuny lamp hangs over the bath, setting the tone. Clothes are hidden behind elegant French dressing screens that would not look out of place in the dressing room of the Moulin Rouge. An abundance of slightly tired lilac drapes over the top of the bucket. A pair of chandelier lamps sits off kilter, adding to the glamour.

Opposite: The serene, elegant, and peaceful bedroom. The bed is unobtrusively screened with voile curtains hanging from tensioned wire. Sera cut the legs off the bed frame to make it less formal and funkier. Bedding is Rachel Ashwell Shabby Chic Couture Petticoat Collection, Crème de la crème.

Overleaf: A Rachel Ashwell Shabby Chic Couture sectional sofa alongside some delicate carved gold chairs is a perfect balance of comfort and elegance. Prom dresses and a hooped skirt lend a theatrical element. A clunky coffee table holds fragrant hyacinths, drippy candles, and well dog-eared books. Light is diffused through vintage, handmade Japanese sudare blinds, which have the appearance of string. All could seem quite serious except for the humorous introduction of a disco ball. Some years ago the roof of the bay window was repaired; it was Sera's chic and shabby choice to leave the rafters exposed. Architectural art!

sera's space

I had recently opened a Rachel Ashwell Shabby Chic Couture store in London when Sera Hersham Loftus and I crossed paths through the small world of interior design. An instant Shabby Chic sisterhood was born. Sera is a stylist and interior designer, creating super-stylish spaces for super-stylish people and sells her own line of beautifully whimsical products. On entering her London home there is a lovely feeling of both a nurturing family nest and a forever-changing Hollywood movie set. The bedroom and en-suite bathroom are in a converted attic. "Out Of Africa" is a core inspiration for her signature Indian screens, which she gessoed for an aged aesthetic and installed throughout. I love the bones of her design. Her mix of shabby frills, the ripped and the wonky, the patina and the history, wilted flowers, and the tarnished bits of bling are a wonderful backdrop for Sera's famous parties.

faded flair

Sera's living room is where rock-'n'-roll meets comfortable family home. Original moldings surround a high ceiling painted khaki to cozy up the room. The floorboards shimmer with many layers of white oil paint—maintenance is a fresh coat now and again. Grand floor-to-ceiling windows with original stripped wood shutters are just beautiful. The ground-floor rooms have been opened up to make a large party room. A traditional mirrored candle sconce transitions to a 1970s silver leather sofa, sitting like a sculpture occupying center stage. Shell macramé lampshades from the Philippines are delicate Sera signature pieces.

Opposite: Authentic debossed radiators frame the entryway along with a baroque clock, playfully greeting guests. Above the entryway is one of Sera's valance designs.

Right: Sera, back in the day, tailored in white. Very much her own woman, sure of her instincts and aesthetic.

Previous page: A relaxed gathering space with functioning aspects. Cupboards built into the niches either side of the stove contain plates and glassware. An abundance of a mellow palette of purple and white lilacs, delphiniums, and hydrangeas truly created a painting. The industrial stove made by Lacanche is both aesthetic and practical.

Opposite and left: The massive concrete sink from an architectural salvage company takes on the qualities of an oversized dressing table, with huge ornate mirrors and linen panels, ribbon-tied onto tension wires. The tough work surface is made from flagstones. I love this strength and beauty. The elegant French armchairs support my philosophy of beauty, comfort, and function.

glamour in the scullery

Down the stairs into the semi-basement kitchen, glamour continues to reign. As with so many homes, this is where friends and family gather. The chairs are well sat-on and the sturdy table is well used. The six lady chairs are unique unto themselves, but slipcovers bring some casual uniformity. The elegant armchairs offer unexpected comfort in the workplace. The parquet floors have been sanded down and stenciled, introducing some formality to plain wooden planks, which adds to the "upstairs" feel of the "downstairs." Sunlight slips through the door leading to the garden; otherwise lighting is discreetly low level, with no harsh overheads to disturb the ambiance. Wuthering Heights is waiting to happen.

Opposite: A real kitchen scullery feeling. A functional sink with evidence of history. The pillar tap allows for large vessels to come and go. Lilacs and delphiniums, even leftover petals, are picture perfect.

Left: A Cinderella story. An elegant dressed "lady chair" sits next to a humble but so very useful milking stool, both of equal importance. Aesthetically and philosophically, I am always wanting to make sure co-stars in my make-believe world get their due credit.

There is a practical aspect in going back in time in the kitchen. In the midst of flower preparations, there is still room in the oversized concrete trough for a metal bowl to hold dishes waiting to be washed. Stone, brick, wood, and metal materials with their individual beauty, complemented with floral arrangements in the making, is an aesthetic that is somehow good for the soul.

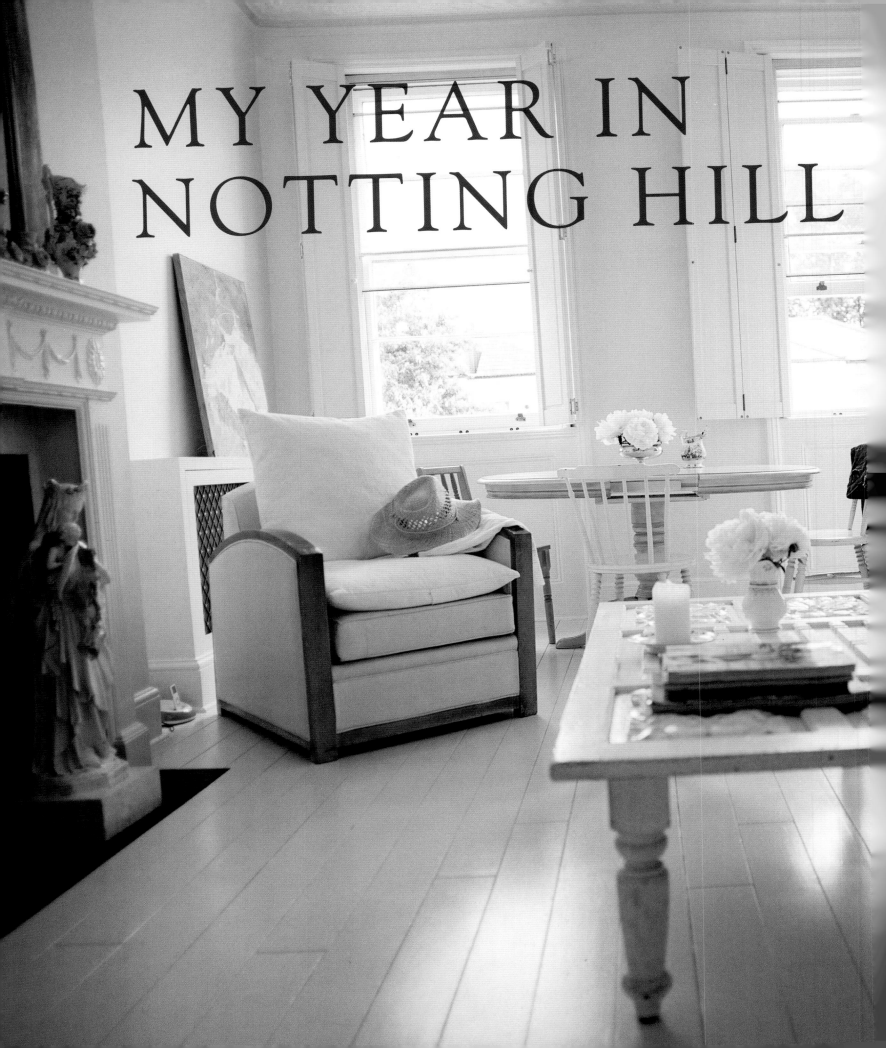

MY YEAR IN NOTTING HILL

Previous page: Checking out vintage treasures at Portobello Market—Friday is the least hectic of the shopping days. My rented living room walks my talk with flowers, candles, and a coffee table improvised from a cupboard door. Sash windows flood the room with light.

Below: Once grand single dwellings, this elegant terrace is typical of the architecture in the more gracious areas of Notting Hill. It's a very buzzy and eclectic place to live, with Portobello Market just around the corner.

Opposite: I added the vintage fire screen—a touch of decadent grandeur. I spent many an inspirational moment looking out of that window to the oh-so-English garden below. I observed the four seasons, from leafless trees to abundant foliage, and I swear I saw Peter Pan and Wendy fly by nightly.

Below: My altar of calm and remembrance on the bedroom mantelpiece. Peonies are among my favorite flowers, exploding from a little jug I picked up at the market.

Opening a store in London was a big adventure for me. I wanted to embrace my English heritage and reinforce the original aesthetics of Shabby Chic. In an effort to immerse myself in the culture of the neighborhood, I made a temporary home for myself in an apartment around the corner from my store. Having lived in California for 30 years, light and space are important to me and big windows and two lovely white armoires created a sense of space and light in what was quite a small room. With my signature calm, comfortable, and beautiful surroundings, I can leave hectic living at the front door. Calm means a white palette and a lack of clutter: I layered in a few of my favorite things and cozied up the landlord's sofa with a dozen Marseille pillows from the store.

Previous page: A chandelier from my store. I often add amber beads or amber-colored shades, as the color is very flattering to skin tones. One of the elements that attracted me to the Notting Hill apartment was the pair of painted, slightly scuffed, very grand French armoires. At vintage markets I buy lots of bling jewelry—sometimes I wear it and sometimes I use it in my design work.

Opposite: The shop's frontage leaves passersby in no doubt as to the style and level of chic to be found inside.

Right: A handwritten note on our doorknob—"back in 5 minutes" is so English! An emotionally resonant needlepoint motto placed for fleeting inspiration. Vibrant pink feathers make an irreverent appearance among a display of pretty china, and a Darcy dining chair from my collection (named for "Pride and Prejudice") with a machine-washable seat cover.

my beautiful boutique

I am really proud of my tiny London store. It is only 850 square feet, but it is a showcase of all that is authentic to my style and values. It is a transatlantic labor of love. Having stores in California, New York, and now London and Texas, I always consider merchandise unique to each location. However, the common thread of aesthetics and values of Rachel Ashwell Shabby Chic Couture runs through all four. As I put together the collection for London, I was careful to balance the Californian spirit of sumptuous, oversized whimsy that is my signature, with the traditional and unique British style.

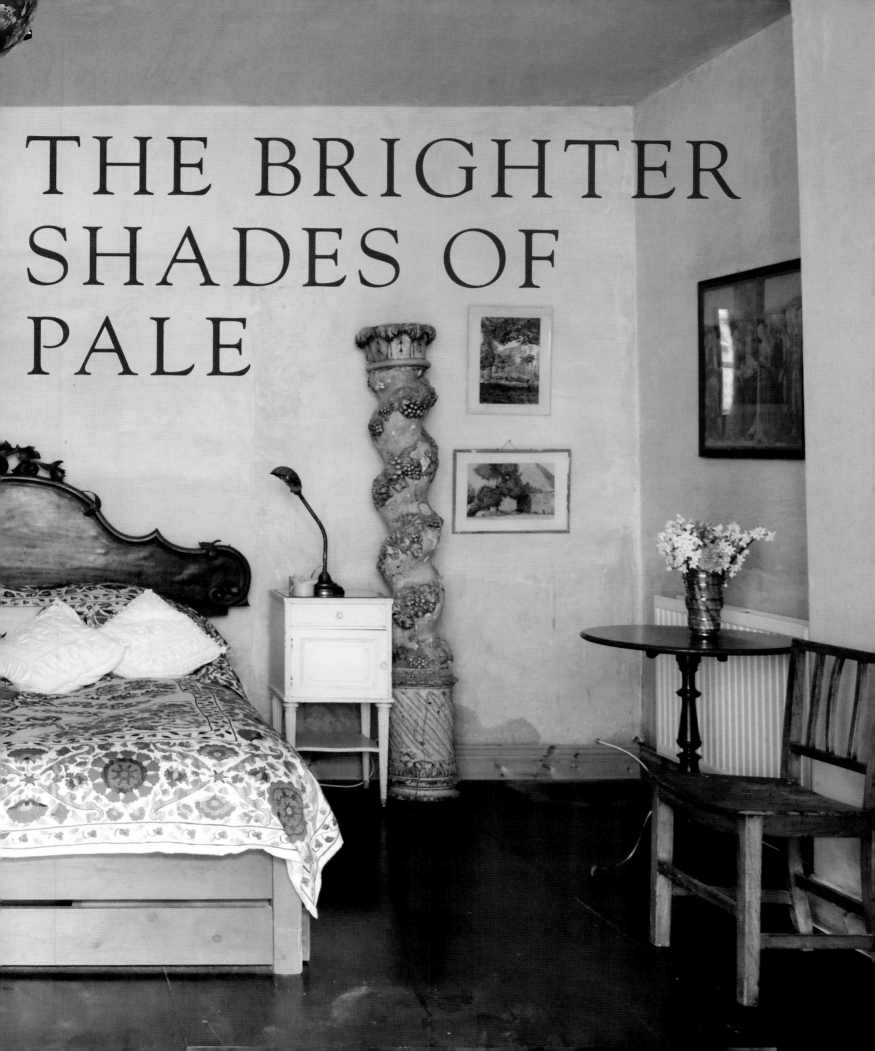

THE BRIGHTER
SHADES OF
PALE

Previous page: Patina, patina, patina. This room could be empty and still lovely. However, Sophie's antique finds of a jewel-colored Turkish bedspread and a cranberry glass shade make the room mystically magical. The bed is a chunky platform painted gray. The bed head is a crown from an elegant armoire, while pillars are 18th-century Italian columns.

Left: A chair from Lots Road Market in London—silk brocade, grandeur fading.

Opposite: An Indian bejeweled glass lamp globe and a mellow worn brass lamp, with an unusual crucifix flicker-flame bulb as a special detail.

Sophie's space

Sophie Muller is one of my oldest childhood friends. As teenagers we would have sleepovers in our London family homes—and now we have our own grown-up homes. I love her home—completely inspirational. She decorates with such confidence, with little interest in "non-colors," which have been the core of my design for so many years. I have recently embraced a smokier, dusty palette but well-traveled Sophie has a bravado with color that escapes me. Her talent for combining meaningful bits and pieces is evident in her aesthetics. The spare room of her home in London's Belsize Park needed replastering, with the intention of repainting, but in the end the unfinished plaster was left beautifully as is. The cool, raw walls have the look of a California mission.

faded raspberry comfort

Decades ago, Sophie and I would share our dreams of "going to Hollywood." In our own ways we have. Sophie has taken her talents all over the world as a credited top director of music videos in the league of Beyoncé, Eurythmics, Gwen Stefani, and Annie Lennox. She's not a rock-'n'-roll person, but working in the music industry has exposed her to bling and glitter with a raw edge, some of which she has introduced into her surroundings in her home. We have similar appreciations of aesthetics and historical inspiration, and it's comforting knowing that we share childhood roots. Sophie has collected wonderful, meaningful bits and bobs on her travels from Lots Road in London to the bazaars of Morocco. She is such a good conveyor of the stories attached to her finds.

Previous page: Sophie's sitting room, much influenced by her travels to Morocco and India, is peaceful in its strength of color, seen in the brave aqua walls, and authentically lived-in, like the threadbare oversized rug. The red leather-bound albums on the coffee table contain press clippings of her playwright father Robert Muller's reviews and journalism—an authentic living memory.

Opposite: A fat, clubby armchair re-covered in raspberry linen. The fake fur cushion covers are falling apart at the seams.

Left: Sophie as a little girl, before we met and shared our dreams.

In her sitting room, her faded raspberry sofa and turquoise walls are captivating. Rich, floral, mushy velvet cushions and a wall of higgledy piggledy books, the glint of mirrors, gilded frames, and sparkling icons—all are so gorgeous, engaging, and welcoming. Sophie reads her books, she lights her fire, she plays her piano, takes inspiration from her household of gods, and doesn't care if the sun fades her sofa. Sophie fully participates in her life and home.

Above: The kitchen dining room is painted a quiet shade of cream—Sophie is not fond of white walls. The show-stopping blue dresser in the kitchen is needed storage and a gift from a friend. Her rather quirky 70s chandelier combined with classic and modern seating are perfect examples of a hodgepodge of designs that can sit comfortably together.

Opposite: Travel mementoes: a glamorous lady mosaic lamp and an Indian print with embroidered embellishments. I love the lampshade with attached gold tassel trim—good tacky!

sophie sleeps here

Travels in Tibet influenced Sophie to feature the stripes of strong color in her bedroom and the simple painted plaster walls. There are also moments of tattered elegance with the crystal-drop wall sconces and mismatched, unrenovated chairs and tables with past stories to tell. As a focal point, or rather a shrine to life, Sophie has placed a freestanding fireplace surround in front of the chimney. A silvered sheep's head looks down on Sophie's magpie collection of memories and treasures. There is such a pleasurable feel in every room of this house of things being used and appreciated.

Previous page: More books and more unexpected choices of style in the main bedroom. The colorful Moroccan quilt picks up the Tibetan palette of the dark paint and the horizontal stripes. A little Florentine night table brings a touch of 18th-century elegance.

Left and opposite: The lovely wonky wall sconce throws shadows on the painted plaster. Propped up on Sophie's mantel are mementos of her life and meaningful icons. The central image is a "thank-you" from Annie Lennox.

GLAMOUR
AND BLING

Previous page: A handmade tablecloth from the Petticoat Collection at Rachel Ashwell Shabby Chic Couture cascades over the dining table. Shimmering silk wallpaper, the soft gleam of well-polished silver, and the glow of candlelight create an artful, glamorous ambience with attitude. Lavender sterling roses in a timeworn silver trophy command center stage, while other floral displays in varying stages of bloom perform meaningful supporting roles.

Left and opposite: To me, perfection: roses bloom and drape as though made from velvet. Soft pink roses, blooming in their peak, nestle in little silver urns. I love the abundant Tiffany-blue silk curtains that casually puddle to the floor. The custom-carved Louis XV chairs in silver-leaf finish were made by a local craftsman.

bling and shimmer

Sharon and Ozzy Osbourne have homes in the US and England accommodating family, friends, and nine dogs. I asked Sharon where home is and she said "everywhere is home." Like me, she has mastered the craft of creating a safe, welcoming haven and accenting beautifully with roses, candlelight, and a bit of bling and shimmer. There are differences of taste to consider between Ozzy and Sharon. Ozzy, of course, is known for his gothic, black, rock-'n'-roll aesthetic, while Sharon loves frills, glitz, and glamour. Somehow the two styles complement each other and find a way to live together.

The dining room of their glamorous Californian home shimmers with diffused light. The hand-painted de Gournay silver-gilded wallpaper with an antique finish is a reference to grand country-house opulence. It's a setting for a great party. The silver and subtle turquoise palette sets the stage for an abundance of bling by way of delicate wall sconces and a treasured family heirloom chandelier that originally held candles. Glass and mirrors keep the light dancing.

Dining rooms are not as commonplace as they once were, but they are such a treat. There's no better place to set a scene and tell a story that fits the company and the occasion, in the way a stage set complements a play. Evidence of memories in the making are everywhere—in the roses on the cusp of wilting, candles dripped down to the end, a crinkled petticoat and lace tablecloth ready for laundering, plates stacked ready to be stored once more in cupboards, and curtains pulled back to let in a glimmer of morning-after daylight.

Above: White lace, cut glass, fine porcelain, and silver. A dinner party is a perfect excuse to bring out the heirlooms.

Above right: Shimmering details on the hand-painted silk paper set the perfect backdrop for a long crystal wall candelabra and a blue silk curtain.

Opposite: The faded elegance of roses in their most perfect state just before decay, candles of dripping perfection, the worn patina of antique mercury glass— a beautiful mess.

Opposite: As grand as this entrance is, there is still evidence of family life and a distinct personality from the moment the door is opened.

Below left: The most traditional little brass wall sconce is layered with a floppy vintage velvet blue flower, a small accent that pulls the story together, quietly and whimsically.

Below center and right: The Osbournes' soap—what a novelty. Heavy metal meets crystal drops. I love the combination of a tea-stained lacy vintage chandelier shade, and a black and white photo of Ozzy from earlier days.

the grand entrance

As the door opens into the Osbournes' home, the first sight of the blend of rock-'n'-roll and Hollywood glamour is evident. The *Gone with the Wind* sweeping black staircase is the backdrop for the soothing subtle palette of blond floors and walls and a pile of lovely creamy vintage luggage awaiting a glamorous journey. Sharon first saw the French porter's chairs in the top-floor restaurant of Bergdorf Goodman in New York and ordered them immediately for her home.

BLISS ON
THE BEACH

Previous page: This pale blue wooden chair is my throne. It may be wonky and the fabric is barely there, but there is no princess who is graced with more treasures than I. Whenever possible, we dry everything on washing lines. These floral frocks and floaty blouses are inspiration in the making.

Opposite: My beloved Savior Table is perfection to me. It is part of our Couture Collection, designed during a time we needed some "saviors!" Made locally in Los Angeles, it's wonderfully practical with extendible breadboard ends; the dry white paint finish is full of character.

Left: The all-important details, authentically complementing the blue and white palette. A much-loved teeny oil painting capturing my favorite colors, including lilac. While I don't drink wine, I so appreciate bottles and labels that "speak" to me. Scrunchy napkins, fresh from the washing line, and the remnants of a vintage hat.

my paradise

Just down the beach from Paradise Cove, Malibu, I found this quirky shack. It was the day-to-day sanctuary I was looking for. Other prospective renters didn't quite know how to work with the hodge-podge layout, but for me the patched-on additions suit my discombobulated life quite well. There is something rather perfect about not knowing how long this will be my "home" but, like the ocean and the endless horizon, the experience is something you cannot own. To furnish this place, I scrambled together bits from my other worlds, and my traveling box of tricks made this instantly into a home with a soul. Having a criteria of beautiful, comfortable, and functional things supports spontaneous decorating. Most pieces were leftovers, but somehow they fit like they were purposefully purchased.

sprawl in comfort

The enclosed seating area next to the deck is a modest 10-foot square with windows both high and low so the space is always flooded with light. No need in having curtains as the view is what this room is all about. Humungous as this sofa is, it comes apart and reconfigures—it has moved five times from homes I have owned and rented. Britney Spears, Pamela Anderson, and my teenage kids

have all lived with this sofa—the tales it could tell! It fulfills the criteria for all my furniture: it is timeless, stylish, and of the very best quality. The room is all rather monochromatic except for the layers of soft red and gold bohemian vintage rugs. I tried putting pictures and paintings on the walls but took them down again, content with propping the images against the window. They looked happier there.

Previous page: A pale, calm, and uncluttered seating area next to the deck. This communal and bright room is the prime interior space in which to "zone out." A well-worn wooden coffee table welcomes sandy feet. A wall-to-wall Rachel Ashwell Shabby Chic Couture sectional sofa, slipcovered in white denim, anchors the space. Laughter and solitude sit equally well here.

Right: An irresistible little armchair from a flea market in Round Top, Texas. The fabric is a thick cream canvas embroidered with tiny glass beads. I think the chair is African in origin. It sits in the corner shimmering quietly in the shadows of the huge sofa, complemented by the yummy duck egg blue cushion.

Far left: A whimsical silver garland wraps around a light fixture.

Left: I created an art installation with sacred hearts and feathers from necessity of having to cover up a bunch of holes I had made in the wall in error. Art by happenstance.

hearts, pearls, and beads

I love to add unexpected elements and little meaningful details to my design work. In the central room of my paradise, I felt the need to pay homage to the vast ocean view with the glimmer of a few special sparkles. I replaced an inherited Tiffany-esque, view-obstructing hanging lampshade with three metal garlands by Tord Boontje. They glint and reflect both daylight and candlelight beautifully. When accepting a home in an "as is" condition, I find it useful to ponder the good qualities, layering in some magic, and possibly the combination is perfect imperfection—similar to that of any relationship in life.

Left: My gratitude candle. I give thanks daily when I light this candle and blow it out at the beginning and end of my day. My list of things to be grateful for is quite long now, but I find the ritual very grounding. My candle sits on an antique holy water stoop from a Catholic church, along with a little happy Buddha of my Mum's and a tiny glass Shiva, the Hindu deity of transformation. Total balance from many powers.

Opposite: Many friends and family members who stay here become captivated by the ensemble that creates this altar of peace and calm. The tablescape consists of two Virgin Marys, another Buddha from my Mum, flowers (of course), a candle, and an old journal I picked up with an evocative oil painting on the cover. The various elements evolved without plan into a very zen, balanced arrangement. The Marys and Buddha have a very definite vibe, with the eye symbolizing being watched over and protected.

Below: My dear friend Kim McCarty has quite a following for her expressive watercolors of children. Alongside hangs an embroidered Serenity Prayer for many situations in life.

Below right: Louis and Rose. I found the enormous overblown roses at a textile show. They were unpackable, so I carried them home to LA in the outside pocket of my Louis Vuitton carry-on bag. They became an airport lounge show-stopper amd conversation piece. During the course of the journey the pair of them struck up a relationship.

Opposite: My desk and my Inspiration Book—my bible, providing fuel for my future endeavors. The white abstract sculpture of mother and child was done by my Mum, who was my greatest influence. Her aesthetic is very much part of who I am, and her gentleness is evident in this piece. The painting of an unknown southern belle which I picked up in Savannah, Georgia, exudes a matriarchal presence.

my creative nook

Above anything else I consider myself an artist, and I believe that creativity cannot be switched on and off during working hours. So wherever I am, I create a workspace to capture my creativity. Where my senses are balanced, my inspiration connects to my art. My mantra—beauty/function/comfort—guides me, and all is well taken care of in this work nook. I don't believe in clutter and I don't trail around the unnecessary. I am a very good editor of "things." If an item is beautiful, functional, and necessary, then it has a place of honor in my home, and I've learnt to pay close attention to things that pass through naturally, like a shell found on a beach or a precious thank-you note. My eyes and heart are always open to meaningful souvenirs of life.

waking with the sun

I have never been one for needing a major master bedroom. As long as there is room for a sumptuous bed, perhaps a squishy comfortable chair, and a table for flowers, then I am truly happy. Living by the beach, I wake with the sun; I just have voile curtains to diffuse the light, and for the larger window I've folded a ripped bedcover over the curtain pole. It feels very organic and natural, like a tent in a charming state of disrepair. A bedroom is where voices of reflection and future plans find space in our minds. More than any other room in the house, it is important to create a feeling of calm, nurture, and safety, and the "less is more" quality of decor supports that thinking for me.

Opposite and above: My favorite way to display roses is with as little stem and as few leaves as possible—it's all about the blooms. Voluspa candles come in lovely glass jars that are "must-keeps." White Whisper bed linen is just as good as it gets: luxurious linen from Belgium, sold through Rachel Ashwell Shabby Chic Couture.

Previous page: My simple, yummy bedroom: pretty, functional, and extremely comfortable. As the giant rosary draped over the mirror proves once again, I am drawn to religious icons, but in an abstract way. For me they represent someone somewhere expressing a moment of faith.

Overleaf: I am always sprinkling my Mum's bit and bobs around, such as this little pink ribbon, a Murano lamp like a pink wave, and a blue velvet tassel that adds a hint of color and stops the curtains slipping off the pole.

lily's room

My daughter Lily was raised in Malibu, and it's a place she will always have in her soul. Although she has lived in New York and in London, she really appreciates this little foothold. I have filled her room with left-over loveliness. The room has some gorgeous knick-knacks of inspiration that Lily may well put into her design work now that she has— surprise, surprise— entered this field.

Life seems to have taken my kids—Jake and Lily—to different parts of the globe, but it is reassuring to know that we have this beachside treasure where we can regroup when time allows. There is something about a beach home that requires little more than people. All else becomes secondary, making the focus just being together. The setting of nature seems to support the reliving of memories, to be in the moment and contemplate the future.

Opposite: Above the chest of drawers is an intriguing painting that fits perfectly into this lovely space. The artist painted her Viennese grandmother from an old photo—the result looks like a snapshot memory.

Right: A detail of the wonderful rubbed and faded paintwork on the chest of drawers that has been decorated with a freehand stencil. The stenciling and the worn paint are a combination I just love.

Above and opposite: An inspirational collection. A pair of cool, icy-textured vases with a splash of pretty pink. A beautiful chaos of flamboyant color and exuberant modeling on a Capodimonte vase.

Left: Lily loves hangers. Padded with silk and satin, beribboned and bowed, the artful confections are as pretty as a picture. They absolutely deserve to be out there and appreciated, not tucked away in a dark cupboard.

Opposite: The floral bedding is part of my Simply Shabby Chic Collection sold at Target stores in the US. Gorgeous, affordable luxury.

Below: A signature, beautifully worn bedside table, full of stories and soul. It felt right to combine a skinny metal lamp base with a lampshade inspired by a Victorian petticoat.

Previous page: The blue tissue bell, a bit faded now by sun and seawater. If it's down, my friends know I'm home and can pop by. The guest cabanas—only half an hour away from my hectic Los Angeles life.

Below: A handful of the perfect palette firecrackers ready for an impromptu celebration. And sunglasses— a vital accessory in this house where the sun shines in everywhere. This house enjoys magnificent light.

space for friends

Friends sleeping over comes with the territory of beach living. I have many sleeping nooks in this house, along with what I call two beach cabanas which are accessed by a spiral staircase. While the furnishings conform to my signature of beauty, comfort, and function, I have kept these rooms low-key in design. Just comfy beds and side tables and a few frills and flowers which, depending on guests, I may de-frill in exchange for some simple crisp sheets.

least but not forgotten

I always pay great attention to bathrooms. Plumbing in Malibu (and, interestingly, in London too, it seems) can sometimes be a challenge, so function and cleanliness are of utmost importance. Sometimes guests are impromptu, unable to tear themselves away at the end of a perfect day, so my bathrooms are always equipped with appealing guest toiletries and other necessities. Sweet-smelling wildflowers and a thought-provoking motto on the wall are tiny gestures that mean a lot, and come summer, even vintage clothes to loan out, if needed.

Above and above right: For unexpected guests, toiletries must always be inviting. (A must is to make sure all caps and bottles are cleaned from the previous guest.) A supply of fresh toothbrushes and mini toothpaste tubes goes down really well. Fresh flowers always say "welcome to my home."

Opposite: Touches of pink and frills add beauty to function. On the wall is a saying by Kenneth Cole, taken from a magazine. "It's amazing what you find if you look in the opposite direction." Food for thought.

dining on the deck

An open trellis dapples the sun onto the open-air eating area. The table and bench are flea-market finds. The chunky teak chairs are leftovers from a garden setting; I made some linen covers to diffuse their heaviness and also as protection from seagull mess. To the ocean end of the deck, the little wicker settee had one broken leg. Rather than fix it, I chopped off the good three—it seemed the simpler solution and now it is a perfect height for viewing the gentle activity of the ocean where dolphins dance along the tops of the waves, and paddle boarders and kayakers glide zenfully by.

Opposite and above: My breezy deck with a view to the sea and the sky—a place for eating, along with projects that find their way out here. (My iPod is tucked around the corner, playing my sappy country music.) For me, a beach house should have wooden floors, but the terra-cotta tiles that came with the house are certainly livable. By day this is a wondrous spot and at night, with candle and moonlight combined with the sound of the sea and the wind, I cannot but think this is a peek into heaven. Flowers are waiting for me to distribute into vases: pink and purple stocks, roses in shades of pink, and white lisianthus are favorites of mine. A detail of one of the floaty dresses hanging on the washing line. All part of the gorgeous scenery.

A LIFE THAT DESIGNED A HOUSE

Previous page: The kitchen is basic and functional. The taps and hardware are simple and ubiquitous; the sink is of vintage soapstone. The one long shelf above the kitchen surface holds all the dinnerware for a family of five. Decorative elements come from the kids' artwork and flowers in various states of bud, bloom, and decay.

Opposite: The McBreens' aesthetic is best described as industrial meets country. There's a hard edge to this well-trodden kitchen/dining space at the hub of this busy household. The "Floatation" ceiling light, by Ingo Maurer, takes away any sentimentality.

Below: Everywhere you look in Brendan and Jeanne's home there are flowers, candles, and pretty things. Among many things, Jeanne collects vintage cotton hankies which are used as napkins.

sharing and caring

Brendan McBreen I count among my dearest and oldest friends. Brendan, now an interior designer, worked closely with me at Shabby Chic for over 20 years. He is steeped in the history and aesthetic of the company. Along with his own sense of decor, he and his wife Jeanne, who also worked at Shabby Chic, own a lot of archive Shabby Chic stuff, but what they did with their home was inspired by their own philosophy. Brendan designed and built a minimal-meets-country barn in Malibu and created within it one communal space with two massive sliding doors that isolate the bedroom spaces, but only at night. Their life is about keeping connected, and it's their house that has created this enviable level of interactivity.

make-believe spaces

The house is divided by two barn doors on tracks. With a family of five, the flow of space and ease of access to everything are vital. Cupboards are few and far between. Dust doesn't have time to settle. In the hallway, communal possessions are piled on open shelves, encouraging a spirit of sharing. In the huge wicker hampers is a lifetime of Shabby Chic fabrics and bed linens. Twenty years' worth of a brand are tucked away in those hampers and in spite of changing times and trends, the fabrics, the patterns, and the colors still pull together. They may be faded by laundering and sun bleaching, but still they sing a lovely song.

Above: Phoebe's bed is a glorious tumble of fabrics from Shabby Chic's past and present.

Opposite: Rio enjoys a quiet moment with a book. There is no television in the house, so the children naturally play creatively and read for pleasure.

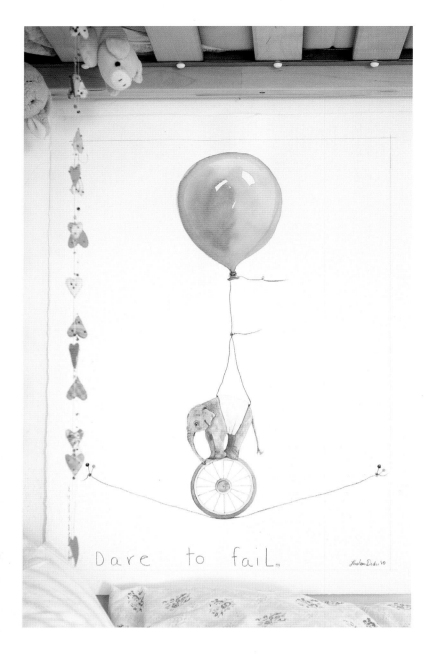

Dare to fail.

Previous page: Wonderfully wonky wicker hampers hold all the household linen, spare duvets, quilts, and pillows. Shabby Chic archival bed linens in familiar stripes and florals have stood the test of time and washing.

Left: "Dare to Fail" by Lisa Dirkes. We sell her whimsical, philosophical, original watercolors in our stores.

Right: The kids' bedroom. Phoebe sleeps on the bottom bunk with the dark pink florals; Owen sleeps on top, and Rio's bed is the pale pink one surrounded by artwork drying on the line.

sleeping and storytelling

The children's bedroom is a lively shared space. Everything is shared, including the one computer—an inspirational thought for big and little people. With three kids, the house can be noisy, but it seems respect for each other's needs has been a lesson learnt through living. Tolerance, compromise, and consideration is just the way it is. The room is a wonderful space, full of love, wit, and wisdom. It's comfortable and casual, too, with squishy velvet beanbags, a fabulous faded vintage rug to pull all the colors together, and a fun prop from a circus—an elephant stand. Many a story to be told from here.

This page and opposite: Phoebe, Rio, and Owen's mom and dad have created a home that inspires creativity as a way of life as opposed to a hobby. Elements that create and support their distinct interests are easily accessible when impromptu ideas pop into their innocent and uncluttered minds. Evidence of this can be seen in charming "artistic moments" throughout the home. My favorite is "the puff ball feathery thing," as described by Rio. Whenever I leave after visiting, I always feel special that I know a family like this—old fashioned in their family values while still so fashion forward in their creativity. Board games, storytelling, sewing, and drawing are intermingled with entrepreneurial ideas and adventures. A balance in life to aspire to.

Previous page and right: Emma's distinctive bicycle. She uses scraps of wonderfully traditional Bennison fabric, chenille bobbles, ribbon, and funky bits of trim that she wets then stretches around the bike frame to dry in place. She customizes bicycles for people who fall in love with the eccentric look.

Left: Emma started experimenting with different types of feathers to create her "Worn with Love" line of headdresses: chicken feathers from her sister's farm, guinea fowl and pheasant feathers from the local butcher, a friend's blue parrot, feathers gifted by Canada geese that romantically fly thousands of miles across the ocean. The end results are beautiful and cherished works of art. Powerful and magical gold-painted wings of flight adorn this headdress fit for a chief.

a world of yesterdays

Emma Freemantle lives in a houseboat moored on a London canal, a lifestyle choice she embraces. It comes with compromises of space and convenience, but the charm and the camaraderie of neighboring houseboat-dwellers are captivating, and the slip-slap of the water and the call of water birds diffuse city-center noise. Emma refers to her home as a cocoon, an igloo (during the snowy months). She is a designer, photographer, and stylist; part of a group of artists drawn to the past and to things beautifully crafted by hand. All of them, I have found, share my philosophy of the beauty of imperfection, celebrating the recycled and the vintage. Emma makes customized bicycles wrapped in scraps of fabric, feathered headdresses and corsages, banners and wall hangings, all with the idea of telling a story through threads and old fabrics and celebrating the imperfections that make a piece unique. "I am constantly sourcing for the unusual, for the unique," she says. "I am drawn to a world of yesterdays, where the artisan was an important member of the community. Things were made to last and the idea of mass consumerism was as distant as the concept of visiting the moon."

Previous page: The main cabin is filled with necessities and treasures. Every square inch is considered, and a constant editing process takes place. Pinned on the walls is eye-catching evidence of a passionate life; photographs, matchbook souvenirs, notes, bits and bobs create the décor.

Opposite top left and right: Emma is a total romantic and gravitates towards beautiful found poetry or words of her own. She has a vintage Corona typewriter that she uses to type directly onto fabric, giving this poem—a compilation of friends' thoughts on love—a beautiful quality.

Opposite top right: I love looking through Emma's styling diaries, full of Polaroids, sketches, and notes documenting past projects and reference for future ideas.

Opposite bottom left: A friend's parrot gifted some blue and yellow feathers, waiting for their day to be transformed.

Opposite bottom right: Emma outside her treasured boat. Emma has crafted for herself a beautiful life. "I would encourage everyone to surround themselves with comfort and beautiful things," says Emma, "It's what my working life is about."

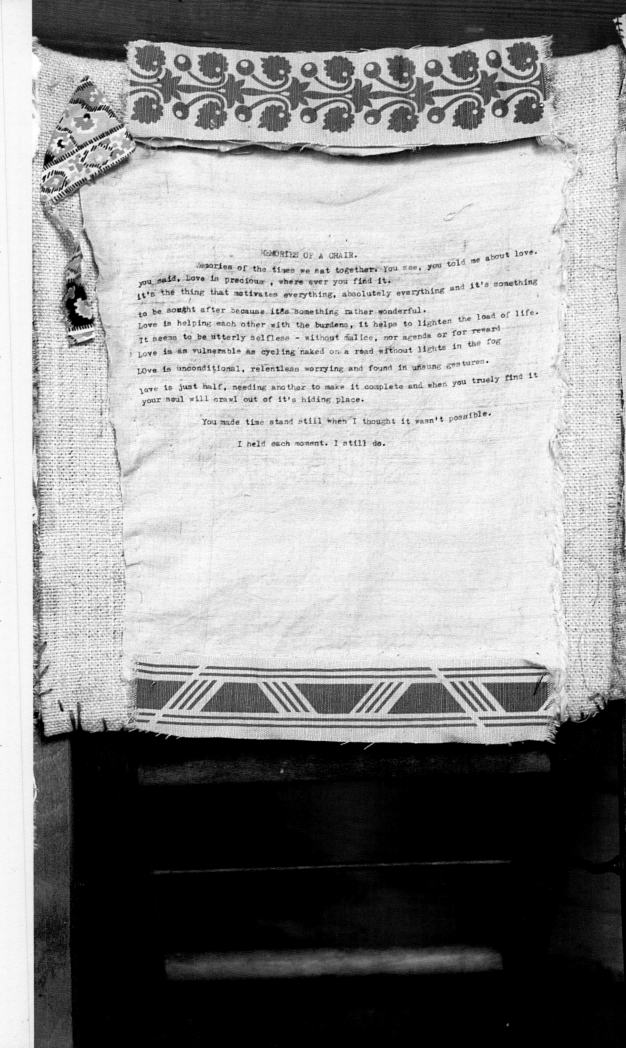

MEMORIES OF A CHAIR.
Memories of the times we sat together. You see, you told me about love.
you said, Love is precious , where ever you find it.
it's the thing that motivates everything, absolutely everything and it's something
to be sought after because it's something rather wonderful.
Love is helping each other with the burdens, it helps to lighten the load of life.
It seems to be utterly selfless - without malice, nor agenda or for reward
Love is as vulnerable as cycling naked on a road without lights in the fog
LOve is unconditional, relentless worrying and found in unsung gestures.

love is just half, needing another to make it complete and when you truely find it
your soul will crawl out of it's hiding place.

You made time stand still when I thought it wasn't possible.

I held each moment. I still do.

PETIT
PALACE

Previous page: The "everything" room with Wilfred the dog and the chair he has commandeered. The painting of roses is universally beautiful in our language, as are the threadbare child's dress hanging on the wall like a fragment of butterfly wing and the sacred hearts above the door—a common thread amongst many of us. Their witty light fittings, including the candelabra with a counterweight of old books, are for sale on their James Plumb website.

Opposite: James and Hannah walk their talk. Laminate, track lighting, and fashionable granite ae not needed in their kitchen. This charmingly shabby room was assembled from old, worn, and well-loved freestanding items piecemealed together into a real cook's treat. Foodstuffs, herbs, and stoneware platters share the higgledy-piggledy shelves with whimsical moments, wild flowers, and vintage glass. Natural daylight creeps into the little room above the old stone sink.

Left: A ballerina humorously and gracefully tucks herself away among kitchen necessities. A lampshade is clipped onto a shelf, more in keeping than something modern.

passion for the timeless

Sometime ago I discovered James Russell and Hannah Plumb when visiting London Design week. Their amazing exhibit of inspiring and original assemblages stood out from the other artists. I knew immediately I had discovered a precious couple and their treasures. They met as fine art students at Wimbledon College of Art. Now home for them is a tiny 1820s house in Stockwell, London, once a priest's house for the church next door. Entering into their lives, their home, and their spirit is a glimpse at life lived in the last century, authentically. In their little historical space, they work at re-purposing things, such as hand-embroidering battered and faded Persian rugs, turning hatboxes into lampshades and silk screens into laminated panels. They describe what they do as discovering potential in the forgotten and beauty in the everyday, which is very much my own philosophy and the ethos behind everything I do. This young couple live their art casually and naturally; it is not a contrived aesthetic. I love crossing their path as we scour the English treasure haunts, comparing our discoveries.

Previous page: The narrow, wonky staircase leads from the kitchen to the upstairs landing and serves as a bookcase on the way. There are stories to tell all over this house. The little "altar" at the top of the stairs displays, under the tissue bell, a postcard of the Taj Mahal. The ribbon marks the spot where James and Hannah drank champagne to celebrate James's 21st birthday. Hannah pinpricked MARRY ME onto the postcard as her proposal and propped the card in front of a candle—a treasured memory now.

Opposite: From the ceiling of their office hangs one of their "luminaries," usually commissioned and sold in multiples of three or five. The room is a typical hodgepodge of artistic inspiration. The striped curtain was once a beach tent.

Above: Beautiful clock faces with no hands, international in thought.

Left: A vintage Christmas tree decoration marries a candle and a radiator.

timeless living

James and Hannah travel the world with their artistic installations. Their work is increasingly sought-after. They have a studio down the road; however, as with all artists, it is hard to contain their projects and art overflows into their home. The tiny room at the top of the stairs is, for now, their office where they sit at their wonky desks with battered painted legs and collaborate on stories to tell, real or imagined. They kickstart ideas with found objects and mood boards pinned up with scraps, cuttings, and memorabilia, causing this space to evolve as their creativity evolves: an ever-changing canvas of life. Office lighting is from sturdy classic Anglepoise lamps, shelves are random planks mounted on cast iron brackets, and discarded elements of trash go into beat-up buckets. I could slip into this workspace easily.

The bathroom is equally old fashioned, sweet, and quaint, but very practical. When visiting, I was drawn to the Virgin Mary candle and, of course, loved the feminine pink blooms, beautifying the raw patinas. Our palettes are quite different, but in James and Hannah's house I feel we come together with soul. Their eye for detail and their reverence for the history of possessions—all this resonates with me.

Left and opposite: Hard to believe that this bathroom is in London's heart, and that the 21st century bustles outside. Stable doors, wooden beams, and sheets of soap hanging from string are all so charming. The walls are scraped back to the original brick, the plumbing and steel bathtub are brand new, the tiles of the panel are deliciously old, and the wooden surround has been covered with beaten lead so the whole bathing visual is beautiful, original, and functional.

Overleaf: Even though the tiny bedroom is lined with washed black linen, there is still a softness and romance to this room. One small sash window with restricted light reflects the slubby white linen bedcover. A bed canopy-once part of a tent- is a typical example of Hannah and James's designs. The tiny flowers in the corners are the unsung heroes.

PEARL'S PLACE

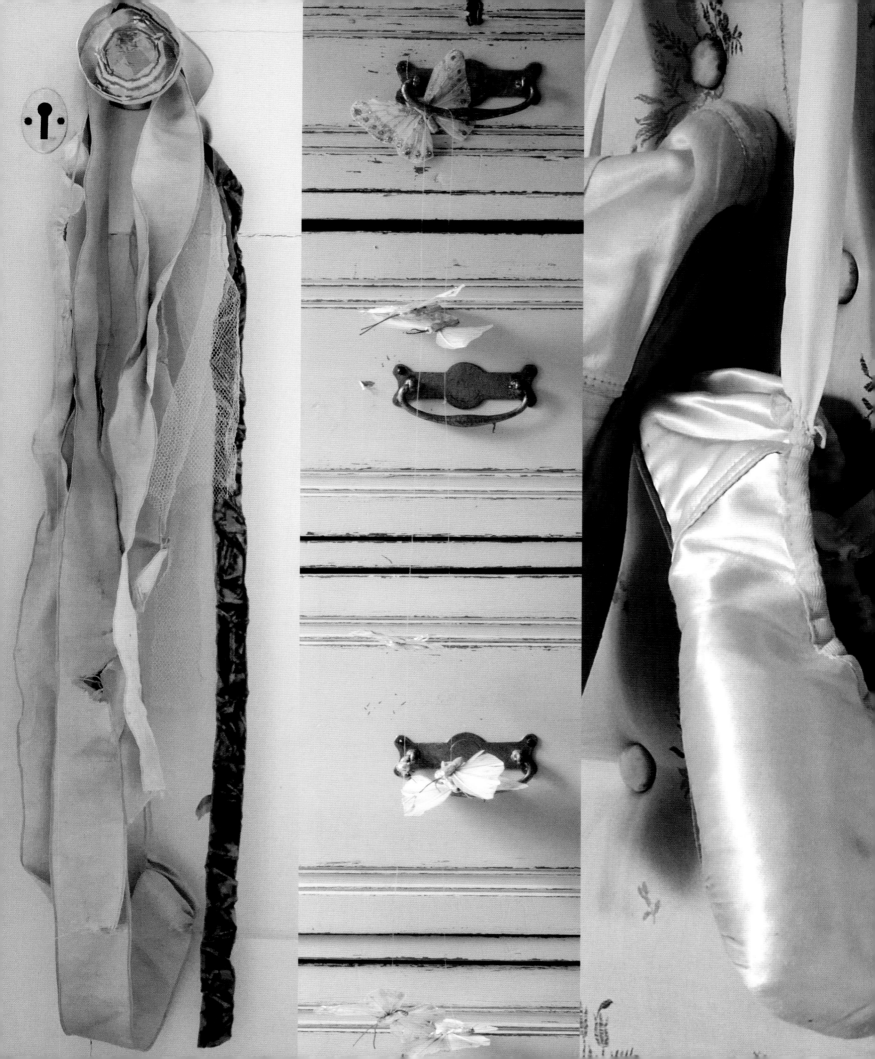

Previous page: In a corner of Pearl and Danny's bedroom sits a friendly threadbare chair with a wonky leg that's surprisingly strong; a perfectly floppy decorative cushion adds to the charm. A clutch of ribbons on a pretty brass doorknob. Butterflies on handles and ballet shoes from Daisy's bedroom.

Right and opposite: Daisy's bedroom is a younger version of her mother's. The room has pretty pink flattering lampshades and a mix of florals and ticking stripes on the bed. In a casual way, an empty but decorated birdcage hangs centrally for aesthetics, while a working chandelier is hung close by for light. This room is orderly, restful, and comfortable; no clutter, only selected personal pretty accessories. I love the blush-pink velvet crown pillow—faded grandeur with its lost stuffing.

a dressing-up box

It takes a lovely drive through the rainy English countryside to Somerset to visit Pearl Lowe at her charming cottage. She lives with her husband Danny Goffey, the Supergrass drummer, and their three children, Alfie, Frank, and Betty. On weekends, her fashion-model daughter Daisy Lowe often returns to the family nest from the hectic pace of young London life. There is a wonderful feeling of dress-up and make-believe in the home, and Pearl's projects all contribute to the creativity that emanates from every room. Children's giggles and the smell of baking complete the vision of a well-balanced home. Pearl Lowe has left behind her Britpop days and is now a fashion and interior designer. After my own heart, her work is inspired by vintage finds. Pearl has a true understanding of my aesthetic, embracing along with the wonkiness and whimsical prettiness her own brand of rock-'n'-roll bling. She describes the interior as the inside of a dressing-up box—I love that thought. Pearl's home explodes with an exuberance of ribbons, silk and lace, gilded butterflies, and ballet shoes.

This page and opposite: Details from Daisy's simple, little-girly pink bedroom that is a retreat from the catwalk and the high life of London, full of pretty things and memories. A fabric heart hangs on the mirrored door of her wardrobe. Beautiful reflections are guaranteed. It seems to me that as sophisticated and quickly as our girls grow up, they still love to know that back at their family home, they can be vulnerable and girly.

Pearl and Danny's bedroom is comfortably opulent. It is an example of Pearl's love of pink (although she likes to accent with black lace). Their bed is a lovely French Empire style—all gilding and scrolls. Bedding is the Rosabelle Collection, with a round pink Petticoat pillow, both from Rachel Ashwell Shabby Chic Couture. At the end of their bed is a purple velvet tufted blanket box, found by Pearl on one of her treasure hunts. The shaggy rugs on the white floorboards add a touch of luxe on a cold, dreary English morning. Pearl loves the whimsy of butterflies, as with the mirror, and feathers always add a touch of make-believe. Pearl and I share many aesthetic similarities, but what connects us more is the philosophy of our design work— gentle, practical, inspiring, nurturing, purposeful. The sisterhood of designing!

gathering place

A large old kitchen farmhouse table accommodates family and friends at meal times. But due to the central position of the kitchen in the home and all the artful projects that take place here, it often transforms into a table of creativity. I always love an open kitchen. Thankfully, gone are the days when the preparation, cooking, and clearing of meals were hidden away from sight.

Above left: A pretty mismatch of chairs, each with a distinct character, and a glamorous chandelier. Pearl enjoys the search for treasures in her local town of Frome. She loves to paint and distress the furniture she finds and marry them up with vintage fabrics when needed.

Above: Pretty, pretty Pearl.

SHABBY
MAN

Previous page: In the corner of Huw's sitting room sits a chair he has no intention of re-doing, along with a Squishy sofa from Rachel Ashwell Shabby Chic Couture, covered with a somewhat rumpled grain linen slipcover—as comfy as a well-worn linen suit—both appropriate for a shabby man. The mislabeled animal print and faded elegant mirrors are from Huw's collection that he creates and sells.

Opposite and left: Huw's kitchen is pure eye candy to me. Installing random panes of colored glass was a priority in his uncontrived restoration of his home. One-of-a-kind mismatched plates and glasses create a lovely story. Cracked mugs still hold flowers, with a small glass liner within to hold water.

Overleaf: A 1940s American wallpaper complements subway tiles totally authentically. Blueberry crates serve as extra storage. Simple, brilliant, and real.

Huw's home

I first became aware of Huw Griffith when I bought one of his artfully distressed 19th-century mirrors with fabric backing. Huw is a designer and stylist who lives in an 1814 town house in Shoreditch, London, crammed with wonderfully mismatched and tattered pieces waiting for his inspiration and attention. His art is to find old things, transform them, and give them a new life. With its striking touches, like the random-colored glass panes and one-off, tattered treasures, his home feels like a Russian folk house, with no contrived decoration and only just enough of anything. His kitchen, seen on these pages, is authentic and atmospheric, with vintage wallpaper, old subway tiles, and beautiful touches of cracked and chipped heirloom crockery.

Previous page: Lovely Huw in his comfortable shabby sitting room, perfectly at ease. The glazed internal door has panes of colored glass, which inspired Huw to echo the jewel-like surprise in his kitchen window.

Opposite: Huw's lucky sweater—he was wearing it the day he met his fiancée Tess—worn to shreds and put in the dryer by mistake. A fond living memory.

Left: Not a self-portrait, but the painting somehow emulates Huw's aura. A feminine but unfussy touch of anemones in a cracked motto jug (lined with a glass to hold water), and ranunculus in a teal-colored shot glass. Love the trio.

Artist in residence

"As far as possible, I don't have an over-abundance of stuff," says Huw. It's a sentiment that resonates. Every surface in Huw's home is a still life. As simply as he lives, every object has innocently earned its place and serves a purpose. Huw's sitting room is both a repository of his work and a testing ground, as well as a place to relax. His house has a lovely period feel. Generous sash windows let in plenty of London light, making the once-elegant shabby furniture, original wood floors, faded rugs, and whimsical chandeliers the perfect backdrop for a designer who draws his inspiration from the past.

Opposite: Prayer mats gathered from flea markets are scattered. A rather fancy floral canvas carries faded flowers up the wall. The overall look is fluid, mussed up without being messy, casually relaxed, and artful.

Below: Inspirations and work in progress. Huw's ledger, and the brand labels in development for his range of apparel and home wares. A frivolous sketch detailing a costume design for the role of Columbine. Oversized motto mugs make for sweet but tough vases. Lovely scented stocks echo the floral painting.

sleeping room

Neither overly masculine nor feminine, Huw's bedroom is eclectic, interesting yet restful, and so very charming. The palette is various shades of cream with pink and blue accents from rugs, flowers, and folded clothes. The chandelier has surprising pink glass drops. The room is sparsely furnished but very welcoming, with basic necessities, along with a vintage dressmaker's form for clothes to be plopped. There is a beautiful sense that everything is just the way it is as Huw comes and goes, and it works.

Opposite: Brown lace, a gray knitted throw, and a ditsy floral sheet make up a lovely rumpled bed from another era. The quilt is a sawtooth 19th-century American design from New England.

Left: On the dairy door hangs one of Huw's extensive collections of vintage T-shirts—elements of inspiration for his creative endeavors, which include a line of skinny oilskin trousers. Such an original genius idea.

I truly love Huw's unique aesthetic. It is intelligent, historical, uncontrived, and so very authentic. He has a masterful eye for pattern and form that extends into everything he owns and touches. It gives me great heart to see artisans living their work honestly and without compromise, affording a rich life of beauty, comfort, function, and memories in the making.

Huw only finds room for the special and meaningful. Fascinating black-and-white family photos, rich with history; a door recycled from an English dairy farm; and a gloriously eclectic folksy feel that's both glamorous and utilitarian.

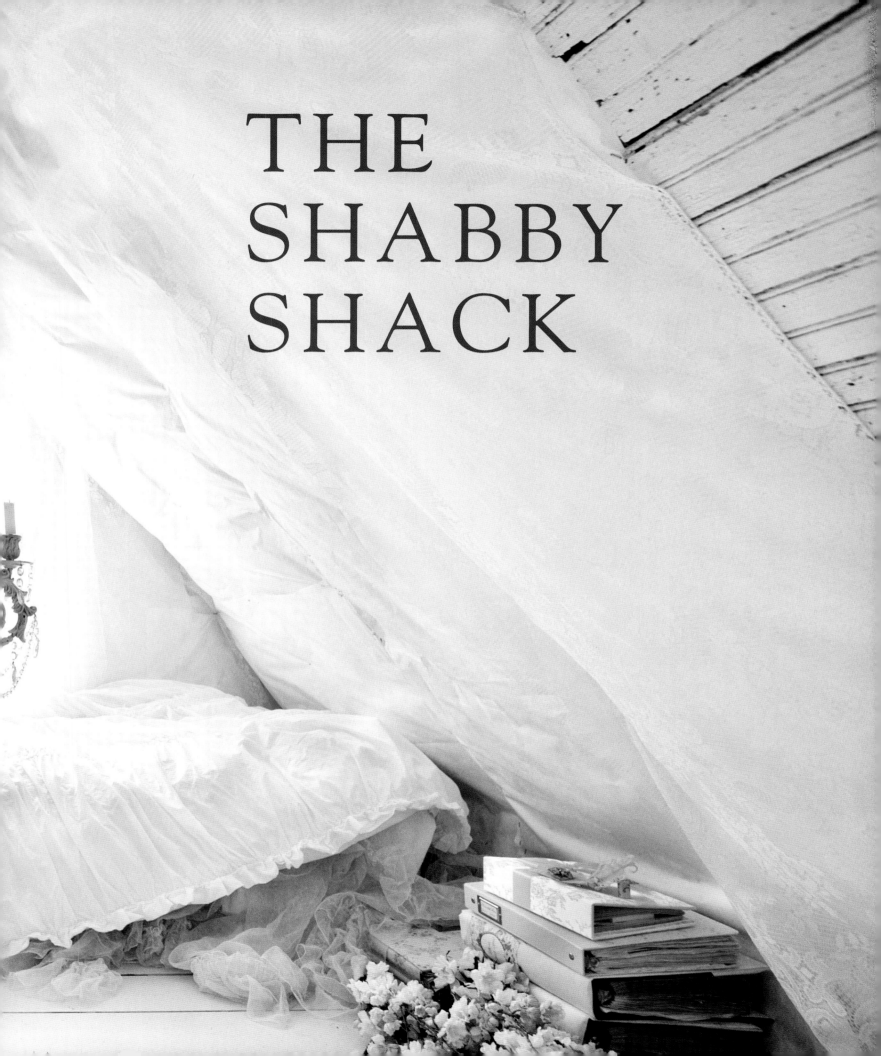

THE
SHABBY
SHACK

white magic

Over a stream and up the hill to the edge of a cool green wood in the Catskill mountains, Sandy Foster has created a tiny romantic gingerbread cottage. Armed with a jigsaw, a vision, her salvage-store finds, and her red rainboots, she turned what was a simple hunter's cabin—just a 9 by 12-foot box with a peaked roof—into her fairytale dream. Creating this haven has been a total labor of love, completed on a shoestring budget. This is Sandy's refuge, her miniature dream home but with no heat, no bathroom, or kitchen. The practical necessities are housed in a trailer that she shares with her husband Todd on the other side of the stream.

Previous page: The sleeping platform was part of the original cabin. Using every square inch of space, Sandy transformed the platform into a fluffy white cloud for her bed. The bedding is from the Simply Shabby Chic collection.

Left: From her doorstep, Sandy collects wildflowers and pops them into an eclectic mix of flea-market glass jars.

Opposite: The picture-perfect cabin and the petunia-filled porch. Sandy found the lovely old windows with their imperfect glass in a salvage shop, and cut into the cabin walls with a jigsaw to install them. The porch door, with its lovely battered hunter green paintwork, is a treasured salvage-store find. The gingerbread trim is all her own work—inspiring.

Overleaf: A perfect shabby and chic interior, a place to sleep, dine, and live. There's even a "library" of vintage books with pastel covers—all heavenly and so clever. Fragile tissue paper garlands round the windows, a $15 flea-market chandelier, and loads of flowers make this a perfectly "edited" little space. The small Ikea wicker sofa is camouflaged with vintage linen sheets and plump pillows.

Previous page: Access to Sandy's world is across a stream and up a steep hill, so the furnishings were either extremely lightweight, or came in bits and were built to fit—like the china cabinet she made using salvaged timber and French doors from a garage sale. It's filled with stacks of nearly-matching Limoges china with a tiny rosebud pattern.

This page and opposite: Where two worlds collide: Inside the "Groove Tube," as Sandy's husband Todd calls his trailer home, in reference to the 1970s avocado and gold color scheme. But even in here there are touches of Sandy's chic: the flaking aqua-painted wooden chairs and the wildflowers in a bottle. On the recycled door hangs a sachet made by a local artist.

both sides of the stream

Sandy's idea of home is cute, picture-perfect, and white. Todd's could not be more different. "Todd likes to collect things and stuff, most of which is very large, like tractors," says Sandy. Owning a dream home has been a longing since childhood, when her father's business collapsed and the family lost their comfortable Long Island house. It was her determination that fueled her vision and her resourceful labor of love that made her dream a reality. I so admire how she quietly and solidly beats to her own drum. And now she has the best of both worlds: a loving husband doing his own thing in his "man cave," and just a trip over the stream away is her picture-perfect dream world of flowers and white calm.

Opposite and left: Together, Sandy and Todd share a love of the gorgeous scenery of the Catskills and the open-air lifestyle. And while Todd collects bits of machinery, Sandy continues to beautify their lives with moments of poetry and her perfectly chosen treasures.

LIVING ART

Previous page: An open workspace has always suited me best. Unless private words are needed, I find everyone feeds off each other better without walls. This is the heart of the creative process. Christmas for us is in August when we brainstorm ideas for gifts and store displays. As winter draws in, we play with the idea of a pastel summer. This is a truly collaborative family.

Left and opposite: Inspiring eye candy complements merchandise, giving both meaning. The hands and flowers from a beautiful, albeit somber, painting of a nun gave me food for thought as I was displaying some rosette brooches on a mellow silver mannequin for a store display.

my creative playground

How lucky am I that this is the space I call my office? This is the home that supports "the village" that supports everything in my world of creating and design. There are about 15 of us that call this our "home of work," from financial to creative to logistical, each role of equal importance. The magic of my product is the soul that touches the process. Many pieces are one-of-a-kind, entirely handmade with dedicated care and consideration. Sewing machines hum over the hammering of nails and the splish-splash of dye buckets: a true melting pot of ingredients making magic.

Opposite: As I walk the fields of flea markets, it is often just a patina that catches my eye. This horse is unusual, as pink and white is not a common palette for a piece such as this. But since the day I found it, I haven't been able to part with it. It's been used for hanging Christmas decorations and now greets guests at The Prairie by Rachel Ashwell.

Right: Religious figures captivate me. Often they are somber, but I am drawn to the ones with a lighter spirit. This flock of saintly women, being white, has an ethereal quality. Noses sometimes need small repairs but I tend to leave other bumps and chips "as is."

UM

HAPPY MOTHER'S DAY

HIRLEY
EENFIE

WEDS. & S
or tel. 770-

says Ashwell. "It's where I go to clear my mind."

SEPTEMBER

MONDAY	TUESDAY	WEDNESDAY	THURSDAY	FRIDAY	S
1	2	3	4	5	
8	9	10	11	12	1
15	16	17	18	19	20
22	23	24	25	26	27
29	30				

Chica

Beauty & the Brid
Vive Glam

SHABBY

EDWARDS

RE

mood boards

Creating a mood board is the initial step in my creative process, and my favorite thing to do. It is the first place I download my vision. It might be through sketches, magazine articles, fabric swatches, or magical embellishments that demonstrate a feeling. I often layer in personal bits and bobs of family photos or handmade notes, just to ground and give my boards substance. The end result is a record of the beginning stages of my vision. As time goes on, I may edit or add a new element, and that is what makes this living art so alive.

Previous page and these pages: This particular mood board was my version of an historic Shabby Chic family tree. As my everyday experiences fall naturally into a cohesive palette, the end result is pleasing to the eye. The trick to the details is using interesting things to attach the layers of papers and fabrics, from simple pins to other little embellishments —like punctuation on the board.

resources

Rachel Ashwell Shabby Chic Couture stores:
1013 Montana Avenue, Santa Monica, CA 90403
117 Mercer Street, New York, NY 10012
202 Kensington Park Road, London, UK W11 1NR
5808 Wagner Road, Round Top, TX, 78954
www.rachelashwellshabbychiccouture.com

Simply Shabby Chic
www.target.com

The Prairie by Rachel Ashwell
5808 Wagner Road, Round Top TX, 78954
www.theprairiebyrachelashwell.com

My blog
www.rachelashwellshabbychic.blogspot.com

Brendan McBreen Design
www.brendanmcbreen.com

Emma Freemantle
www.wornwithlove.co.uk

James Russell & Hannah Plumb
www.jamesplumb.co.uk

Sera Hersham-Loftus
www.seraoflondon.com

Pearl Lowe
www.pearllowe.co.uk

Huw Griffith
www.huwgriffith.com

Sandy Foster
www.myshabbystreamsidestudio.blogspot.com

Lisa Mann Dirkes
www.lisamanndirkes.com

Covent Garden Market
www.newcoventgardenmarket.com

Los Angeles Flower District
www.laflowerdistrict.com

Country Roads Antique
www.countryroadsantiques.com

A Beautiful Mess
www.abeautifulmessantiques.com

The Agoura Antique Mart
www.agouraantiquemart.com

Gisela Torres
www.giselatorres.co.uk

Farrow & Ball
www.farrow-ball.com

Studio Tord Boontje
www.tordboontje.com

Laurence Amelie
(tutu paintings featured on front cover)
sold via www.rachelashwellshabbychiccouture.com

Lamps-on-Line
(crucifix bulb seen on page 63)
www.lamps-on-line.com

de Gournay
(handpainted wallpaper, as featured on endpapers)
www.degournay.com

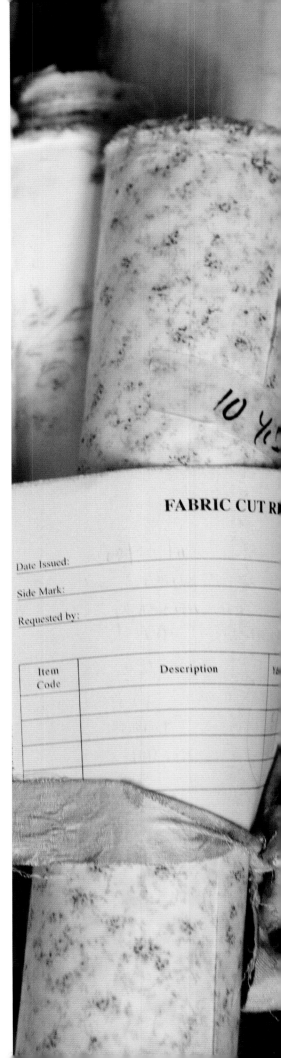

index

homage to a flower

Would I have the knowledge of a flower

That of knowing just what colour I should be

What shape to take and where and when to be these things

As well as that

How long to stay and when to change that form

To draw my petals close as darkness falls

And open myself to the sun's seductive warmth

And then

And then to know

Now is the time to shed that shape and colour

My naked centre breathing soft until another Spring.

(I found this poem written on a piece of paper and signed by my Mum,
Shirley Greenfield. Am not sure if she wrote it or loved it, but it moved me.)

BOCA RATON PUBLIC LIBRARY, FLORIDA

3 3656 0588435 9

747 Ash
Ashwell, Rachel.
Shabby chic inspirations and
beautiful spaces

MAR   2012